My God,
Your God,
Our God

Cover image by Giuliano Ferri
Cover design by Uwe Stohrer Werbung, Freiburg
Book design by Uwe Stohrer Werbung, Freiburg

Originally published in German: Franz Hübner, *Mein Gott, dein Gott, unser Gott*, illustrated by Giuliano Ferri copyright © 2016 Verlag Herder GmbH, Freiburg im Breisgau.
English translation copyright © 2019 by Paulist Press. Translated by Alex Rahn.

Library of Congress Cataloging-in-Publication Data
Names: Hübner, Franz, author. | Ferri, Giuliano, illustrator.
Title: My God, your God, our God / Franz Hübner ; illustrated by Giuliano Ferri.
Other titles: Mein Gott, dein Gott, unser Gott. English
Description: New York : Paulist Press, 2019.
Identifiers: LCCN 2018042722 | ISBN 9780809167890 (hardcover : alk. paper)
Subjects: LCSH: God—Juvenile literature. | Religions—Relations—Juvenile literature. | Religious tolerance—Juvenile literature.
Classification: LCC BL473 .H8313 2019 | DDC 201/.5—dc23 LC record available at https://lccn.loc. gov/2018042722

ISBN 978-0-8091-6789-0 (hardcover)

Published by Paulist Press
997 Macarthur Boulevard
Mahwah, New Jersey 07430
www.paulistpress.com

Printed in China by Printplus Ltd.
April 2019

MY GOD, YOUR GOD, OUR GOD

Franz Hübner

Illustrated by Giuliano Ferri

Paulist Press
New York / Mahwah, NJ

Preface

My God, Your God, Our God is about the ever-relevant subject of tolerance among religions.

Just as Ibrahim wonders which God is the best from the ones people believe in all over the world, many children today face this question at school and among friends.

The story of David, Ibrahim, and Johanna strives to be food for thought and the start of discussion for families, social workers, and teachers. It shows an example of tolerance in a world where a bad sense of multiculturalism not only causes problems among different religions, their attitudes, and morals, but also raises questions for children.

This book points out what unites us on our quest for God. And it demonstrates that behind what seems like differences among various religions, there are people all over the world that long for the same thing: a God who reveals all that is good, beautiful, and loving.

David, Ibrahim, Johanna, and their quest for God can help children discover the commonalities despite differences, especially in families and in school. The story shows that anybody can try to understand and accept another person's faith.

This story can accompany children of all nations on their path to discovering their own God and the God of their neighbors.

This story can help fight rejection and misunderstanding, and foster understanding, friendship, and tolerance.

It seeks to show that all of us—no matter what we call our God—can be friends who value and understand each other.

Franz Hübner

David, Ibrahim, and Johanna had been friends for many years.

They were together whenever possible, wandering through the meadows and fields of their village and sharing many an adventure. They spent time playing, making music, or talking about God and the world.

The subject of God, however, kept dividing them again and again, because the idea of God is a tricky one.

Some people think that they have the best God.

David thought like this.

Some people think that everyone must believe what they believe.

Johanna thought like this.

Some people think that there is only one God.

Ibrahim thought like this.

"I'm tired of us constantly arguing," Johanna said one evening.

The others agreed, because each of them wanted to be at peace with the others instead of fighting all the time.

After a long debate on how to find out which God is the best, Johanna had the idea of going on a journey to look for the greatest God in the whole world.

One of them would travel around the countries of the earth to find the answer.

Ibrahim said he would be willing to solve the mystery—the mystery of who is the very greatest, best, and most powerful God in the world. Together with his mule, Fidelio, and with a backpack full of supplies, he left for his journey. If he had to, he would travel the whole world to find the answer.

Ibrahim was a calm person, someone who looked at the world around him with open eyes, sharp ears, and great curiosity.

During his journey he came to a lake. It shone with a beautiful blue-green color in the midday sun. Full of joy, Ibrahim watched the water's surface where the sparkling sunbeams seemed to dance.

"Who do you think created such a beautiful lake? Which God gave this lake its beauty?" he asked a young fisherman passing by.

The young man frowned and responded, "What a strange question. *My* God created this lake, of course. Because my God is the very greatest!"

And he wanted to convince Ibrahim to believe in his God.

"Thank you," said Ibrahim, and he continued on his way.

Soon Ibrahim encountered a vast forest. After a long hike, he sat down on the soft, warm forest floor.

There was a wonderful scent of fresh green fir and pine resin in the air, and the tall, craggy trees stretched up like powerful, long-necked statues toward the bright blue sky.

"What a magnificent forest," thought Ibrahim, and he watched the play of shadows that the sun painted on the ground through the branches.

"Who do you think created such a beautiful forest? Who is the God that lends it power and majesty?" he asked a passing woman.

The woman reflected for a moment and responded, "Why do you ask such silly questions? Everybody knows the answer: Our God, the God of this country, created this forest. Because our God is the very, *very* greatest."

And she spoke of her God, of whom Ibrahim had never heard anything before.

"Thank you," said Ibrahim, and he continued on his way.

And Ibrahim reached yet another country. Since he had walked a long distance that day, he decided to rest on a ridge. While unpacking his bread, he felt a soft breeze blowing through his hair. It was as if the wind was bringing him the lovely scent of the purple lavender fields below. He saw this cool, refreshing air as a gift from the heavens.

"Who do you think created this breeze? Who is the God that lends it its tender force and makes it so wonderfully refreshing?" he asked a peasant who was passing by.

The peasant responded with a deep voice, "Who else could it be? It is our God. Because our God is the very, very, *very* greatest."

And he spoke of his God, of whom Ibrahim had never heard in all his life.

"Thank you," said Ibrahim, and the next morning he continued on his way.

Ibrahim wandered all day long. It was very hot, the sun seemed to burn in the sky, and the air flickered above the dusty sand.

His mule, Fidelio, trotted slower and slower, and Ibrahim became tired and hungry from the long walk.

Then he found a small oasis with fresh water for Fidelio and himself, surrounded by palm trees full of delicious dates.

How sweet, how delicious that fruit tasted after a long and hard day! He ate one after the other slowly and with joy.

"Who do you think created these delicious dates? Who is the God that provides such good food for us?" he asked the caravan leader who had brought his camels to the water.

The caravan leader replied, "Our great, all-powerful God created these dates, just as he created this oasis and the whole world."

And he described his God, about whom Ibrahim had never heard anything.

"Thank you," said Ibrahim, and he prepared a spot to sleep for the night. That night he admired the shining, starry sky and wondered how his friends were doing at home. He longed to be with them, talking to them and laughing with them.

Ibrahim continued his journey the next morning. And he wandered around for many days, weeks, and months, and still there was nobody who could convince him of who might be the very, very, very greatest God on this earth.

But Ibrahim was grateful for having seen so much beauty. In every country of the world there was something that its people loved and admired. And he started to wonder if maybe there was only one God everywhere, who created all the beauty and magnificence in the world.

The sun started to sink lower in the sky, and the days became shorter and cooler. One day it snowed for the first time, and that night Fidelio and Ibrahim sat freezing and tired behind a wooden shack, eating their meager dinner. Fidelio gnawed stale carrots while Ibrahim ate leftovers from the day before.

Then, a pair of friendly shepherds invited the two to follow them. And so Ibrahim soon found himself in the house of those shepherds, who offered to share their crispy lamb roast.

A warm fire flickered in the fireplace, and Fidelio seemed to get along well with the sheep.

At first, Ibrahim wanted to ask which God had created the fire. But that night he was too tired to ask the same old question.

He thought about these two happy shepherds who took care of him as if he had been their best friend for years. And he was grateful for the warm milk they gave him to drink.

They asked him where he was going, and he told them about the many people he had asked about God. They smiled.

After a while, one of the shepherds, whose name was Gunnar, brought out a guitar and played cheerful songs. Ibrahim felt more comfortable than he had been in a long time.

And when the two offered to let him stay for a while, he accepted gratefully.

They wandered through the surrounding fields and sat by the fire for
hours at a time, recounting their adventures or singing along with Gunnar's
guitar. Ibrahim was grateful for having met such wonderful friends, and
that they had accepted him so dearly. In his heart he was a rich man
because he had learned so many things on his journey, and he had become
friends with these two simple shepherds.

At the same time, after being away for so long, he longed for his friends back home, for David and Johanna. He felt that friendship was the key to their original question.

He realized that wherever people are filled with love, there dwelled the same God. Ibrahim looked thoughtfully at the fire and thought to himself, "God is always the same. Everywhere. In that faraway country where I have been, people called God the one who created the beautiful blue-green lake. In that other country they called God the one who created the wonderful pine tree forest. And it is the same God that created the lavender-scented breeze and the sweet dates in the faraway desert."

He looked gratefully to the two happy shepherds, with whom he felt so comfortable, and suddenly he knew that friendship, too, was a gift from God.

"Yes, in every person, in every beautiful thing of nature I can see God, and God gave us all these things out of love and friendship," he thought. "It is always the same God. Some call God one thing, and others another. I firmly believe that."

And Ibrahim was happy that he had finally solved the mystery.

That night, as he lay in his room, he could not fall asleep for a long time. He was thinking about what he had found out about God. Now he was completely sure that it had always been the same God who had created the many miracles on his journey, including the miracle of his friendship with the two shepherds, who were very dear to him.

Ibrahim enjoyed life with the two shepherds, and every night he thanked God, who was always the same, for each one of those wonderful days. But he longed more and more for his friends back home and could not wait to tell them what he had seen and learned. So he left the next morning to make his way back to his village.

After a long journey, he finally returned home with Fidelio and his nearly empty backpack. His friends ran toward him, overcome with joy.

They had watched for him and were very happy to finally see him again.

But most of all they wanted to hear what Ibrahim had discovered about the very best God.

"I have met many a person who said that their God was the very, very greatest," Ibrahim began.

"Now tell us, which one is the greatest? It's mine, right?" David asked.

"Yes, yours is also the greatest, the *very* greatest, because I believe that your God is the same as the God of all people," responded Ibrahim, his face beaming.

He was so happy and grateful that he was reunited with his friends.

David and Johanna were confused that Ibrahim no longer wanted to argue with them. But Ibrahim embraced his friends and said, "Isn't it wonderful that we have such a magnificent friendship over so many years? You know, I think that if the wind blows in all countries, if the water is wet in all countries, if the dates are sweet in all countries, and if friendship is such a precious gift everywhere in the world, why should we argue over whose God is best? Because if everything is the same across all countries, then the God who created each of these things can only be the one and the same God."

That night, they sat together for a long time around the fire as Fidelio lay on a mountain of fresh hay, gnawing a fresh carrot, and Ibrahim told his friends about his long journey.

And suddenly, David understood: his God is in some ways identical to Ibrahim's God and Johanna's God. Because it is God who, in every country in the world, gives to people the gift of enjoying the beauty of this earth and living friendships. Wonderful friendships just like the one shared between these three happy friends.